HOW TO INVEST

BEST INVESTMENT PLANS 2023

By

KYLIE GREENER

DISCLAIMER

TABLE OF CONTENTS

ABOUT THE AUTHOR

Kylie Greener is an economic consultant specializing in job research and financial strategy. Besides authoring a variety of books on economics, finance, and strategy. She has taught graduate-level courses at a variety of Universities in the US. and China and is currently involved in the MBA Programme at Bellevue University in the US. She has assisted major organizations from around the world in their development for strategic resource management, including the U.S. Department of Defense, the American Red Cross, Ocean Audit, Inc. in the Czech Republic and Saving Humanity in Australia.

PART 1

INVESTING

Investing differs from trading in that it is done for the long term, usually years or decades. Investing is a key strategy for accumulating long-term wealth and financial security.

What exactly is investing?
Investing, in general, is the process of putting money to work on a project or undertaking for a set period to generate positive returns (i.e., Profits that are greater than the initial investment). It is the act of allocating resources, usually capital (money), with the expectation of generating income, profit, or gains.

One can invest in a variety of endeavors (directly or indirectly), such as using money to start a business or purchasing real estate in the hopes of generating rental income and/or reselling it later at a higher price.

Investing differs from saving in that the money is put to use, which implies that there is some implicit risk that the related project(s) will fail, resulting in a financial loss. Investing differs from speculation in that the latter does not put money to work but rather bets on short-term price fluctuations.

KEY TAKEAWAYS

* Investing entails directing capital (money) toward projects or activities that are expected to yield a profit over time.

* The type of returns generated is determined by the project or asset; for example, real estate can generate both rents and capital gains; many stocks pay quarterly dividends; and bonds typically pay regular interest.

* Risk and return are two sides of the same coin in investing; low risk usually means low expected returns, whereas higher returns are usually accompanied by higher risk. Investors can choose to do it themselves or hire a professional money manager.

* Whether purchasing security is considered investing or speculation is determined by three factors: the amount of

risk taken, the holding period, and the source of returns.

Understanding Investing

The goal of investing is to grow one's money over time. The expectation of a positive return in the form of income or price appreciation with statistical significance is the fundamental premise of investing. The range of assets in which one can invest and earn a return is quite broad.

In investing, risk and return go hand in hand; low risk generally means low expected returns, while higher returns are usually accompanied by higher risk. Basic investments such as Certificates of

Deposit (CDs) are considered low-risk; bonds or fixed-income instruments are considered higher on the risk scale, while stocks or equities are considered riskier. Commodities and derivatives are widely considered to be among the riskiest investments available. One can also invest in something practical, such as land or real estate, or something delicate, such as fine art and antiques.

Within the same asset class, risk and return expectations can differ greatly. A blue-chip on the New York Stock Exchange, for example, will have a very different risk-return profile than a micro-cap on a small exchange.

The returns generated by an asset are determined by the asset type. Many stocks, for example, pay quarterly dividends, whereas bonds typically pay interest quarterly. Different kinds of income are taxed at different rates in many jurisdictions.

In addition to regular income, such as dividends or interest, price appreciation is an important component of return. The total return on investment can thus be defined as the sum of income and capital appreciation. According to Standard & Poor's, dividends have contributed nearly one-third of the total equity return for the S&P 500 since 1926, while capital gains have contributed two-thirds.

Capital Gains- are thus an important aspect of investing.

FAST FACTS

Economists consider investing and saving to be two sides of the same coin. This is because when you save money by depositing it in a bank, the bank then lends that money to individuals or businesses who want to borrow it and put it to good use. As a result, your savings are often someone else's investment.

Various types of Investments

Nowadays, investment is most commonly associated with financial instruments that enable individuals or businesses to raise and deploy capital to firms. These businesses then rake in the capital and invest it in growth or profit-generating activities.

While the world of investments is vast, the following are the most common types of investments:

Stocks

When a person purchases stock in a company, he or she becomes a fractional owner of that company. Shareholders are owners of a company's stock who can participate in its growth and success through stock price appreciation and regular dividend payments made from the company's profits.

Bonds

Bonds are debt obligations issued by government, municipal, and corporate entities. When you purchase a bond, you are purchasing a portion of an entity's debt and are entitled to periodic interest payments as well as the face value of the bond when it matures.

Funds

Funds are pooled instruments managed by investment managers that allow investors to invest in stocks, bonds, preferred stock, commodities, and other assets. Mutual funds and exchange-traded funds, or ETFs, are two of the most popular types of funds. Mutual funds do not trade on exchanges and are valued at the end of the trading day; ETFs, on the other hand, trade on stock exchanges and are valued continuously throughout the trading day, just like stocks. Mutual funds and ETFs can either passively track indices like the

S&P 500 or the Dow Jones Industrial Average, or they can be actively managed by fund managers.

Investment Trusts

Trusts are another type of pooled investment. Real Estate Investment Trusts (REITs) are among the most popular in this category. REITs invest in commercial or residential properties and distribute rental income to their investors regularly. REITs trade on stock exchanges, giving their investors access to instant liquidity.

Real Estate

You can invest in real estate by purchasing a house, a building, or a plot of land. Real estate investments vary in risk and are affected by a wide range of factors, including economic cycles, crime rates, public school ratings, and local government stability.

People who want to invest in real estate without directly owning or managing property should consider purchasing shares in a real estate investment trust (REIT). REITs are companies that generate income for their shareholders by investing in real estate. They have historically paid higher dividends than many other assets, such as stocks.

COMMODITIES

Commodities include agricultural products, energy products, and metals such as precious metals. These assets are typically raw materials used in industry, and their prices are determined by market demand. For example, if a flood disrupts the wheat supply, the price of wheat may rise due to scarcity.

Purchasing "physical" commodities entail stockpiling quantities of oil, wheat, and gold. As you might expect, most people do not invest in commodities in this manner. Rather, investors purchase commodities through futures and options contracts. Commodities can also be purchased through other securities such as ETFs or by purchasing stock in companies that produce commodities.

Commodities are potentially high-risk investments. Futures and options investing frequently involve trading with borrowed funds, which increases your risk of loss. As a result, purchasing commodities are typically reserved for more experienced investors.

Mutual funds and ETFs

Mutual funds and ETFs invest in stocks, bonds, and commodities using a specific strategy. When you buy shares in funds like ETFs and mutual funds, you can invest in hundreds or thousands of assets at once. Mutual funds and ETFs are less risky than individual investments due to their ease of diversification.

While both mutual funds and ETFs are types of funds, they operate in slightly different ways. Mutual funds buy and sell a wide range of assets and are frequently actively managed, which means that investment professional chooses what they invest in. Mutual funds frequently attempt to outperform a benchmark index. Because of this hands-on management, mutual funds are generally more expensive to invest in than ETFs. ETFs may also hold hundreds or thousands of individual securities. Rather than attempting to outperform a specific index, ETFs typically attempt to replicate the performance of a specific benchmark index. Because of this passive investing strategy, your investment returns will almost certainly never exceed the average benchmark performance.

ETFs typically cost less to invest in than mutual funds because they are not actively managed. Furthermore, historically, very few actively managed mutual funds have outperformed their benchmark indexes and passive funds over the long term.

Investing Alternatives

Hedge funds and private equity are examples of alternative investments. Hedge funds get their name from the fact that they can hedge their investment bets by going long and short on stocks and other investments. Private equity allows businesses to raise funds without going public. Hedge funds and private equity were traditionally only available to wealthy investors who met the criteria for "accredited investors" based on their income and net worth. Alternative investments, on the other hand, have been introduced in fund formats that are accessible to retail investors in recent years.

Derivatives and Other Options

Derivatives are financial instruments whose value is determined by another instrument, such as a stock or an index. Options contracts are a popular derivative that gives the buyer the right, but not the obligation, to buy or sell a security at a fixed price within a specified period. Derivatives are typically leveraged, making them a high-risk, high-reward proposition.

Investing Style Comparison

Let's compare two of the most common investing styles:

* **Active versus passive investing**: The goal of active investing is to "beat the index" by actively managing the investment portfolio. Passive investing, on the other hand, advocates a passive approach, such as purchasing an index fund, in recognition of the fact that beating

the market consistently is difficult. While both approaches have advantages and disadvantages, in practice, few fund managers consistently outperform their benchmarks to justify the higher cost of active management.

* **Growth vs. value**: Growth investors prefer to invest in high-growth companies, which have higher valuation ratios such as Price-Earnings (P/E) than value companies. Value investors seek companies with significantly lower PEs and higher dividend yields than growth investors because they may be out of favor with investors, either temporarily or permanently.

PART 2

How to Approach Risk and Investing

Different investments carry varying degrees of risk. Taking on more risk means your investment returns will grow faster, but you will also have a higher chance of losing money. In contrast, lower risk means that you will earn profits more slowly, but your investment will be safer. Gauging your risk tolerance is the process of determining how much risk to take on when investing. You probably have a higher risk tolerance if you are willing to accept more short-term ups and downs in your investment value in exchange for the possibility of higher long-term returns. On the other hand, a slower, more moderate rate of return with fewer ups and downs may make you feel better. In that case, your risk tolerance may be lower.

Financial advisors generally advise taking on more risk when investing for a long-term goal, such as retirement. When you have years or decades before you need your money, you are in a better position to recover from drops in the value of your investment.

For example, despite experiencing several short-term lows, including recessions and depressions, the S&P 500 has still provided average annual returns of around 10% over the last 100 years. However, if you needed your money during one of those downturns, you could have suffered losses. That is why, when investing, you must consider your timeline and overall financial situation.

Risk and diversification

Regardless of your risk tolerance, diversifying your investments is one of the best ways to manage risk. You've probably heard the expression "don't put all your eggs in one basket." In the world of investing, this is known as diversification, and the right level of diversification results in a successful, well-rounded investment portfolio.

Here's how it goes: If stock markets are doing well and rising steadily, for example, parts of the bond market may be falling. If you concentrated your investments in bonds, you could lose money; however, if you were properly diversified across bond and stock investments, you could limit your losses. By diversifying your investments across different companies and asset classes, you can offset losses in one area with gains in another. This ensures that your portfolio grows steadily and safely over time.

How to Make an Investment

DIY Investing
The answer to the question of "how to invest" comes down to whether you are a Do-It-Yourself (DIY) investor or prefer to have your money managed by a professional. Because of the low commissions and ease of executing trades on their platforms, many investors who prefer to manage their own money have accounts with discount or online brokerages.

DIY investing, also known as self-directed investing, necessitates a fair amount of education, skill, time commitment, and emotional control. If these characteristics do not accurately describe you, it may be better to enlist the assistance of a professional to manage your investments.

Investing Under Professional Management

Wealth managers typically look after the investments of investors who prefer professional money management. As a fee, wealth managers typically charge a percentage of assets under management (AUM). While professional money management is more expensive than managing one's own money, such investors are willing to pay for the convenience of delegating research, investment decisions, and trading to an expert.

Robo Advisor Investing

Some investors choose to invest based on recommendations from automated financial advisors. Roboadvisors, which are powered by algorithms and artificial intelligence, collect critical information about the investor and their risk profile in order to make appropriate recommendations. Roboadvisors provide a cost-effective way of investing with services similar to those provided by a human investment advisor with little to no human intervention. With technological advancements, robo advisors can do more than just select investments. They can also assist people in developing retirement plans and managing trusts and other retirement accounts, such as 401(k)s.

How Can I Begin Investing?

Getting started with investing is relatively simple, and you don't need a lot of money either. Here's how to figure out which type of beginner investment account is best for you:

* If you have a small amount of money to start an account but don't want the hassle of picking and choosing investments, you could start investing with a robo-advisor. These are automated investing platforms that help you invest your money in pre-made, diversified portfolios that are

tailored to your risk tolerance and financial goals.

* If you prefer hands-on research and picking your own investments, you could open an online brokerage account and hand-pick your own investments. If you're new to investing, keep in mind the simple diversification provided by mutual funds and ETFs offers

* If you prefer a hands-off approach to investing with the assistance of a professional, speak with a financial advisor who works with new investors. A financial advisor can help you build a relationship with a trusted professional who understands your goals and can help you choose and manage your investments over time.

Regardless of how you choose to begin investing, keep in mind that it is a long-term endeavor and that you will reap the greatest benefits by consistently investing over time. That means sticking to an investment strategy whether markets are up or down.

A Brief History of Investing

While the concept of investing has been around for millennia, investing in its current form can be traced back to the 17th and 18th centuries, when the development of the first public markets connected investors with investment opportunities. The Amsterdam Stock Exchange was founded in 1602, and the New York Stock Exchange (NYSE) in 1792.

Investment in the Industrial Revolution
People amassed savings that could be invested as a result of the Industrial Revolutions of 1760-1840 and 1860-1914, fostering the development of a sophisticated banking system. Most of the established banks that dominate the investing world, such as Goldman Sachs and J.P. Morgan, were founded in the 1800s.

Investing in the 20th century
The twentieth century saw the development of new concepts in asset pricing, portfolio theory, and risk management, which broke new ground in investment theory. Many new investment vehicles, such as hedge funds, private equity, venture capital, REITs, and ETFs,

were introduced in the second half of the twentieth century.

The rapid spread of the Internet in the 1990s made online trading and research capabilities available to the general public, completing the democratization of investing that began more than a century before.

Investing in the 21st Century

The dot.com bubble, which created a new generation of millionaires through investments in technology-driven and online business stocks, ushered in the twenty-first century and may have set the stage for what was to come. Enron's bankruptcy, which bankrupted the company and its accounting firm, Arthur

Andersen, as well as many of its investors, took center stage in 2001.

The Great Recession (2007-2009), when an overwhelming number of failed investments in mortgage-backed securities crippled economies around the world, was one of the most notable events of the twenty-first century, if not history. Well-known banks and investment firms failed, foreclosures skyrocketed, and the wealth divide widened.

The twenty-first century also opened up the world of investing to newcomers and unconventional investors by saturating the market with low-cost online investment companies and free-trading apps like Robinhood.

Investing vs. Speculation

The purchase of a security is classified as investing or speculation based on three factors:

* **The level of risk**: Investing typically entails less risk than speculation.
* **The investment's holding period**: Investing typically involves a longer holding period, often measured in years; speculation typically involves much shorter holding periods.
* **Return source**: Price appreciation may be a minor component of investment returns, whereas dividends or distributions may be a major component. Price appreciation is the most common source of returns in speculation.

Given that price volatility is a common risk indicator, it stands to reason that a traditional blue-chip is far less risky than a cryptocurrency. Thus, purchasing a dividend-paying blue chip with the intention of holding it for several years qualifies as investing. A trader, on the other hand, who buys a cryptocurrency with the intent of flipping it for a quick profit in a couple of days is clearly speculating.

Example of Investment Return

Assume you bought 100 shares of XYZ stock for $310 and sold it for $460.20 a year later. What was your approximate total return, excluding commissions? Keep in mind that XYZ does not pay out stock dividends. (($460.20 - $310)/$310) x

100% = 48.5% would be the result of Capital gain

Assume that XYZ paid out dividends during your holding period, and you received $5 per share. Your total return would then be 50.11% (capital gains: 48.5% + dividends: ($500/$31,000) x 100% = 1.61%).

PART 3

How Can Investing Help My Money Grow?

Investing is not limited to the wealthy. You can make small investments. For example, you could buy low-cost stocks, deposit small sums into an interest-bearing savings account, or save until you reach a certain amount to invest. If your employer provides a retirement plan, such as a 401(k), start small and gradually increase your investment. If your employer participates in matching, your investment may have doubled.

Start investing in stocks, bonds, and mutual funds, or open an IRA. Starting with $1,000 is not a bad place to start. A $1,000 investment in Amazon's initial public offering in 1997 would be worth millions today. This was largely due to a series of stock splits, but it does not change the result: monumental returns. Savings accounts are available at most financial institutions and typically do not require a large investment. Savings accounts aren't known for their high interest rates, so shop around to find one with the best features and the best rates. You can invest in real estate with $1,000, believe it or not. Although you may not be able to purchase an income-producing property, you can invest in a company that does. A real estate investment trust (REIT) is a business that invests in and manages real estate in order to generate profits and income. You can invest $1,000 in REIT stocks, mutual funds, or exchange-traded funds.

Is Investing Like Gambling?

No, gambling and investing are very different. Investing involves putting your money into projects or activities that are expected to generate a positive return over time - they have positive expected returns. Betting on the outcomes of events or games is referred to as gambling. Your money is not being invested in any way. Gambling usually has a negative expected return. While an investment may lose money, this is due to the project failing to deliver. Gambling, on the other hand, is entirely based on chance.

In conclusion

Investing is the process of distributing resources into something in order to generate income or profit. The type of investment you choose will most likely be determined by your goals and risk tolerance. In general, assuming little risk yields lower returns, and assuming high risk yields higher returns. Stocks, bonds, real estate, precious metals, and other assets can all be invested in. Cash, assets, cryptocurrency, and other forms of payment can all be used to invest. Stocks, bonds, mutual funds, and real estate are all different types of investment vehicles with varying levels of risk and reward.

Investors can invest on their own or hire the services of a licensed and registered investment advisor. Technology has also enabled investors to receive automated investment solutions via robo advisors. The amount of consideration, or money, required to invest is largely determined by the type of investment as well as the investor's financial situation, needs, and goals. Many vehicles, however, have reduced their minimum investment requirements, allowing more people to participate.

Regardless of how or what you decide to invest in, research your target as well as your investment manager or platform. One of the best pieces of advice comes from veteran and accomplished investor Warren Buffet, who says, "Never invest in a business you do not understand."

Things to Think About Before Investing

Given recent market events, you may be wondering whether you should make changes to your investment portfolio. The SEC's Office of Advocacy and Investor Education is concerned that some investors, including bargain hunters and mattress stuffers, are making rash investment decisions without taking their long-term financial goals into account. While we cannot tell you how to manage your investment portfolio in a volatile market, we are issuing this Investor Alert to provide you with the information you need to make an informed decision. Consider the following factors before making any decision:

1. **Make a personal financial plan.**
Before making any investment decisions, sit down and examine your entire financial situation, especially if you've never created a financial plan before.
The first step toward successful investing is determining your goals and risk tolerance, which you can do on your own or with the assistance of a financial professional. There is no guarantee that your investments will yield a profit. However, if you learn the facts about saving and investing and implement an intelligent plan, you should be able to gain financial security and enjoy the benefits of money management over time.

2. Examine your risk-taking comfort zone.

Every investment involves some degree of risk. If you plan to buy securities, such as stocks, bonds, or mutual funds, it's critical that you understand the risk of losing some or all of your money before you invest. Securities, unlike deposits at FDIC-insured banks and NCUA-insured credit unions, are typically not federally insured. You may lose your principal, or the amount you invested. This is true even if you buy your investments from a bank. The potential for a higher investment return is the reward for taking on risk. If you have a long time horizon for your financial goals, you are more likely to make more money by carefully investing in asset categories with higher risk, such as stocks or bonds, rather than limiting your investments to assets with lower risk, such as cash equivalents.

Investing in cash investments, on the other hand, may be appropriate for short-term financial goals. Individuals investing in cash equivalents are most concerned with inflation risk, which is the risk that inflation will outpace and erode returns over time.

Federally Insured Deposits at Banks and Credit Unions – It's simple to determine whether your deposits are backed by the full faith and credit of the United States government. Go to www.myfdicinsurance.gov for bank accounts. Visit http://webapps.ncua.gov/Ins/ to access credit union accounts.

3. Consider an appropriate investment mix.

An investor can help protect against significant losses by including asset categories with investment returns that fluctuate depending on market conditions within a portfolio. Historically, the returns on the three major asset classes – stocks, bonds, and cash – have not moved in tandem. Market conditions that cause one asset category to perform well frequently cause another asset category to perform poorly. By investing in multiple asset classes, you reduce the risk of losing money and smooth out your portfolio's overall investment returns. If the investment return on one asset category falls, you'll be able to offset your losses in that asset category.

Furthermore, asset allocation is critical because it has a significant impact on whether you will meet your financial goals. If you do not include enough risk in your portfolio, your investments may not earn a sufficient return to meet your objectives. For example, if you're saving for a long-term goal like retirement or college, most financial experts agree that you should include at least some stock or stock mutual funds in your portfolio.

Lifecycle Funds — Some mutual fund companies have begun offering a product known as a "lifecycle fund" to accommodate investors who prefer to use one investment to save for a specific investment goal, such as retirement. A lifecycle fund is a diversified mutual fund that automatically switches to a more conservative mix of investments as it approaches a specific year in the future, known as its "target date." A lifecycle fund investor selects a fund with the appropriate target date based on his or her specific investment goal. All asset allocation, diversification, and rebalancing decisions are then made by the fund's managers. A lifecycle fund's name will most likely refer to its target date, making it easy to identify. Lifecycle funds may have names like "Portfolio 2015," "Retirement Fund 2030," or "Target 2045."

4. Exercise caution when investing heavily in shares of the employer's stock or any individual stock.
Diversifying your investments is one of the most important ways to reduce the risks of investing. It goes without saying: don't put all your eggs in one basket. You may be able to limit your losses and reduce the fluctuations of investment returns by selecting the right group of

investments within an asset category without sacrificing too much potential gain.

If you invest heavily in shares of your employer's stock or any individual stock, you will be exposed to significant investment risk. You will most likely lose a lot of money if that stock performs poorly or the company goes bankrupt (and perhaps your job).

5. **Establish and maintain an emergency fund.**

Most wise investors put enough money in a savings product to cover an emergency, such as unexpected unemployment. Some people save up to six months of their income so that they know it will be there for them when they need it.

6. Pay off high-interest credit card debt.
There is no investment strategy that pays off as well as, or with less risk than, simply paying off all high-interest debt you may have. If you owe money on high-interest credit cards, the best thing you can do in any market condition is to pay off the balance as soon as possible.

7. Think about dollar cost averaging.
By following a consistent pattern of adding new money to your investment over a long period of time, you can protect yourself from the risk of investing all of your money at the wrong time. You will buy more of an investment when its price is low and less of it when its price is high if you make regular investments with the same amount of money each time. Individuals who typically contribute a lump sum to an IRA at the end of the

calendar year or in early April may want to consider "dollar cost averaging" as an investment strategy, especially in a volatile market.

8. Take advantage of "free money" from your employer.
In many employer-sponsored retirement plans, the employer will match some or all of your contributions. If your employer provides a retirement plan and you do not contribute enough to receive the maximum match, you are foregoing "free money" for your retirement savings.
Keep Your Money Working — In most cases, a workplace plan is the most effective way to save for retirement. Before borrowing from your retirement plan, carefully consider your options. Use a 401(k) debit card only as a last resort. Borrowing money now will reduce the

amount of savings available to grow over time and, ultimately, what you have when you retire. You may also face legal consequences (pay federal income taxes and penalties) if you do not repay the loan.

9. Consider rebalancing your portfolio on a regular basis.

Rebalancing means returning your portfolio to its original asset allocation mix. You will ensure that your portfolio does not overemphasize one or more asset categories by rebalancing, and you will return your portfolio to a comfortable level of risk.

Maintain Your Plan: Buy low and sell high – Shifting money away from a performing asset category and into a performing asset category may be difficult, but it can be a wise move. By reducing the current "winners" and

increasing the current "losers,"
rebalancing forces you to buy low and sell
high.

You can rebalance your portfolio based on
the calendar or on the performance of your
investments. Many financial experts
advise investors to rebalance their
portfolios on a regular basis, such as every
six or twelve months. The calendar serves
as a reminder of when you should consider
rebalancing, which is an advantage of this
method. Others advice rebalancing only
when the relative weight of an asset class
increases or decreases by more than a
predetermined percentage. The benefit of
this method is that your investments will
alert you when it is time to rebalance. In
either case, rebalancing works best when
performed on a regular basis.

10. Avoid situations that could lead to fraud.

Scammers, like everyone else, read the headlines. They frequently use a widely publicized news item to entice potential investors and make their "opportunity" appear more legitimate. Before investing, the SEC recommends that you ask questions and verify the answers with an unbiased source. Before investing, always take your time and consult with trusted friends and family members.

Conclusion

We covered real option concepts and the strategic action framework in this chapter. The key points are as follows:
* It is frequently difficult, if not impossible, to justify an investment in certain projects, particularly "exploratory" or "experimenting" or learning projects, using financial techniques such as discounted cash flow, NPV, and economic value added. This is nicely illustrated by the "Jin Beans Tonic Elixirs" case. Under the conditions of uncertainty and irreversibility, businesses should keep their options open and develop a portfolio of investment opportunities.
* Firms can postpone "commitment" under conditions of uncertainty and irreversibility. This way of thinking can

have a significant impact on a company's strategy, including portfolio decisions, mergers and acquisitions, governance decisions, and technology adoption decisions, among other things.

* In order to build a portfolio of investment opportunities, firms must constantly monitor risk, assess market trends, and try new things on a small scale.

Making an investment decision is never simple. Positive or negative cash flows are fraught with uncertainty. It is never easy to choose the appropriate discount rate, but it has a significant impact on the go/no-go decision. Technical analysis based on discounted cash flow techniques does not reduce uncertainty and does not allow for hunches or intuition. One student mentioned that his presentation in another class was graded poorly because he had a gut feeling that a company should invest in a project despite the fact that the NPV analysis was unfavorable. After a brief discussion, I let him in on a great secret revealed to me by one of my mentors after I had spent days attempting to justify a modest expenditure using return on investment calculations. He instructed me to tinker with the numbers until they produced the desired result. Unless the data is manipulated, investment in emerging technologies and a new product line rarely results in positive NPVs. Real options, when combined with the development of a product and project portfolio, can bring truth, beauty, and enlightenment into the investment process. Real options concepts can be used in a variety of ways. Smaller organizations can concentrate on learning by investing in education, reading high-tech magazines and trade publications, attending trade shows, and attending research conferences. Larger organizations can use real options as the foundation for learning, as well as invest in basic research and use learning-by-doing strategies to develop prototypes. The key is to keep one's options open and to build a portfolio of investment opportunities. Monitoring risk and frequent monitoring and assessment of the product and project portfolio by a cross-functional team of key personnel who understand and are aligned with the business mission are important activities included in portfolio development.

Acknowledgement

First and foremost, I would like to express my heartfelt gratitude to Almighty God for allowing us to successfully complete this Business Plan. Then I'd like to thank Dr. John Gray, our honorable supervisor and lecturer at the College of Tourism and Hotel Management, who has always encouraged us to create an appropriate Business Plan, as well as those friends who have provided me with vital information to create this Business Plan. We would like to thank our creator for allowing us to finish our work, particularly for assisting us during difficult times. After overcoming all obstacles and adversity, we have finally arrived at our destination. We are pleased to announce that we have completed our business plan report. Without a doubt, we would like to state that ample knowledge and experiences were obtained during the completion of this course. Though it is undeniably difficult for us to complete the task, it is worthwhile and we learn a lot. We are grateful to the Almighty God for His divine guidance, which has enabled us to complete our business plan.

We would like to thank the Author of this Book Miss Kylie Greener, our entrepreneurship walkabout, for her guidance, support, and advice. She also shares her knowledge and experience to ensure that we complete this business plan on time in accordance with the requirements for the completion of HPD 228.

Recalling our experiences while working on this report, we were able to create a strong bond of friendship among our team members. The strong bond that has been formed and the cooperation that exists greatly assist us in achieving our goals. All of our teammates play critical roles in our success.

We'd also like to thank our family, especially our parents, for their patience and encouragement, as well as our grandparents for praying for us through thick and thin.

We dedicate this work to everyone who is always eager to learn, has the courage to keep studying, and believes in God and Allah at all times.